Vix
Endogo book 8

Published by Crossbridge Books
Worcester
© Crossbridge Books 2025

All rights reserved. No part of this publication may be reproduced stored in a retrieval system, or transmitted in any form or by any means – electronic, mechanical, photocopying, recording, or otherwise – without prior permission of the copyright owner.

ISBN 978-1-916945-17-3

British Library Cataloguing Publication Data. A catalogue record for this book is available from the British Library.

Vix

Endogo book 8

by R M Price-Mohr

Vocabulary for book 8:

aye-aye
because
come
dark
don't
frightened
hear
hole
just
knocking
know
making
moonlight
noise
now
other
out
sleep
think
what

Foreword for teachers

These books have been developed for older beginner readers. The research-based approach focuses on the recognition of just 100 key words that together make up approximately two-thirds of all reading matter in English. By the time the reader has learnt to recognise all the words in book 6, they will know 36 words that make up 33% of all reading matter in English written narrative.

For each new book, twenty new words are introduced and listed at the beginning of each book The new vocabulary for each book should be introduced to the learner in such a way that they will be able to recognise them at sight <u>before</u> reading the book. It is recommended that this is achieved through playing with the printed words. In the first instance, this should be by having two sets of printed and separated words in large font (minimum 20 point) that the beginner reader can match. It is crucial that the teacher continuously verbalise the words, and they may point to significant features in words, firstly the initial letters and secondly to any other distinctive features, to assist with the matching. Following this, the word recognition can be reinforced in games such as bingo, dominoes, snap, Pelmanism etc.

Some temptations to continue to avoid:

- Do not ask the reader to sound out all the individual letters of a word – only the initial letter has value at this stage for reading.
- Do not test the reader to see if they can recognise any of the words by telling you what they say – this should become obvious during the games; remember that visual recognition is not the same thing as verbalising what is seen.

This is Vix the endogo.

It is dark. The other endogos are asleep.

Vix cannot sleep because she can hear a noise.

She is looking out, but it is too dark.

Vix wants to find out what is making the noise.

She is going to get Max to help her.

"I want to find out what is making the knocking noise," said Vix.

Max is happy to help Vix. They go out into the dark.

They can see because there is moonlight.

Now Max can hear the knocking too.

"What can it be?" said Vix. She is frightened.

"I think I know what it is," said Max.

Max goes to a hole in a tree. "You don't need to be frightened," said Max. Vix follows him.

"Come and look," said Max. "It is just an aye-aye."

"Now I can see," said Vix. "It is knocking for food."

High Frequency Words:

because
come
don't
just
now
other
out
think
what

Word patterns:

_out	out	kn_	know
	about		knocking
_ight	moonlight	_ing	making
	frightened		knocking
_ee_	sleep		looking
	asleep		eating
	see		going
	seen		climbing
	green		having
	tree		
	keep		
	been		
	needs		

www.ingramcontent.com/pod-product-compliance
Lightning Source LLC
LaVergne TN
LVHW010315070426
835510LV00024B/3400